Catholic Update
guide to
Prayer

MARY CAROL KENDZIA,
Series Editor

Franciscan
MEDIA
Cincinnati, Ohio

RESCRIPT

In accord with the Code of Canon Law, I hereby grant my Imprimatur
the Catholic Update Guide to Prayer by Mary Carol Kendzia, series editor.

Most Reverend Joseph R. Binzer
Vicar General and Auxiliary Bishop
of the Archdiocese of Cincinnati
Cincinnati, Ohio
June 3, 2013

The Imprimatur ("Permission to Publish") is a declaration that a book or pamphlet is considered
to be free from doctrinal or moral error. It is not implied that those who have granted the
Imprimatur agree with the contents, opinions or statements expressed.

Scripture passages have been taken from New Revised Standard Version Bible, copyright ©1989
by the Division of Christian Education of the National Council of the Churches of Christ in the
U.S.A., and used by permission. All rights reserved.

Cover and book design by Mark Sullivan
Cover image © istockphoto | kjekol

LIBRARY OF CONGRESS CATALOGING-IN-PUBLICATION DATA
Catholic update guide to prayer / Mary Carol Kendzia, series editor.
pages cm
Includes bibliographical references.
ISBN 978-1-61636-674-2 (alk. paper)
1. Prayer—Catholic Church. 2. Catholic Church—Doctrines. I. Kendzia, Mary Carol.
BV210.3.C38 2013
248.3'2—dc23
2013018833ISBN 978-1-61636-674-2

ISBN 978-1-61636-674-2

Printed in the United States of America.
Printed on acid-free paper.
13 14 15 16 17   5 4 3 2 1

Contents

About This Series

The Catholic Update guides take the best material from our best-selling newsletters and videos to bring you up-to-the-minute resources for your faith. Topically arranged for these books, the words you'll find in these pages are the same clear, concise, authoritative information you've come to expect from the nation's most trusted faith formation series. Plus, we've designed this series with a practical focus—giving the "what," "why," and "how to" for the people in the pews.

The series takes the topics most relevant to parish life—e.g., the Mass, sacraments, Scripture, the liturgical year—and draws them out in a fresh and straightforward way. The books can be read by individuals or used in a study group. They are an invaluable resource for sacramental preparation, RCIA participants, faith formation, and liturgical ministry training, and are a great tool for everyday Catholics who want to brush up on the basics.

The content for the series comes from noted authors such as Thomas Richstatter, O.F.M., Lawrence Mick, Leonard Foley, O.F.M., Carol Luebering, William H. Shannon, and others. Their theology and approach is grounded in Catholic practice and tradition, while mindful of current Church practice and teaching. We blend each author's style and approach into a voice that is clear, unified, and eminently readable.

Enrich your knowledge and practice of the Catholic faith with the helpful topics in the Catholic Update Guide series.

Mary Carol Kendzia
Series Editor

Introduction

In March of 2013, a little over an hour after the white smoke arose above St. Peter's Square to announce the election of a new leader of the Catholic Church, Pope Francis stepped onto the Vatican balcony dressed in white to address the roaring crowds and a joyous, excited worldwide audience.

At that moment, when Catholics and non-Catholics alike awaited the hopeful words of the new pontiff, he, in a quiet and humble voice, calmly asked for the people's prayers. "Let's pray always for each other. Let's pray for the whole world. May there be a great brotherhood," Pope Francis said in Italian, wishing that the "voyage with the Church that we begin today" be "successful in spreading the Gospel."

But then, at this most exhilarating moment, the pope brought a hush over the crowd when, bowing his head, he asked those present there in Rome and those watching on television, listening on the radio, or following on mobile devices and computers, "let us pray silently in this prayer for me." Pope Francis then recited the Lord's Prayer, the Glory Be, and the Hail Mary before making the Sign of the Cross in blessing over the crowd.

What was it that caught the attention and caused the quiet of those who gathered at St. Peter's Square? Pope Francis knew at that moment, at that time of a new beginning in the history of the Church, that the successful mission of "spreading the Gospel" is not the work of one person alone but only people joined with God in community. In his first moment as pontiff, Francis taught that God is present if only we have the eyes to see and the ears to hear (see Mark 8:18).

We are sometimes like radios or television sets that are not properly tuned in to a station or channel. The newscasters and entertainers are out there talking or singing away. The station is beaming forth live signals. But if we have not dialed in to the station or our reception of that signal is off, there's no communication.

This is often how it is in our relationship with God. God is out there—as well as inside us—beaming forth his love and goodness, but it's lost on us because we fail to pray; that is, we fail to tune in or open ourselves to God's loving presence.

The *Catholic Update Guide to Prayer* is an invitation to a richer prayer life, an invitation to answer the deepest call of the human heart to find union with God. It's an invitation for each of us to seek and embrace God in the space of our everyday lives.

Our search for God in prayer is not restricted to special times and places. The Holy Spirit invites us, in the words of St. Paul, to "pray without ceasing" (1 Thessalonians 5:17). To pursue this call, it's important to have a balanced attitude about the world in which we find ourselves.

Almost anything we see or experience can be a prayer—a pathway or tool for tuning in to God. There is a whole spectrum of ways that can raise us to conscious union with God: passages of Scripture, repetition of words, silence, breathing, even suffering. Such experiences become springboards and passageways into God's presence. The same could be said of walking or running or watering plants or gazing into a child's face.

We need to discover ways to remind ourselves of God's loving presence in our everyday world. God is present to us twenty-four hours a day. In this little book, we will look at ways to heighten our awareness of God and access our ability to pray at any time, in any place.

CHAPTER ONE

The What and Why of Prayer

Whether we know it or not, we are already in the presence of God and united with God because God is everywhere—within us and without.

St. Francis of Assisi saw all creatures as stamped with God's image and as stepping-stones to the Creator. For him, every creature and earthly experience—sun, moon, wind, air, water, fire, earth, animal, plant, and even "Sister Bodily Death" (as in his "Canticle of the Creatures," also known as the *Laudes Creaturarum*)—was a window to God in a world that is charged with the "grandeur of God," in the words of the poet Gerard Manley Hopkins.

Prayer helps us bring to consciousness this precious bond we have with God and his saving love. As Trappist monk Thomas Merton pointed out: "In prayer we discover what we already have…. We already have everything, but we don't know it and we don't experience what we already possess…. The whole thing boils down to giving ourselves in prayer a chance to realize that we have what we seek. We don't have to rush after it. It is there all the time, and if we give it time it will make itself known to us."

As Merton points out, we are not aware of the union with God we already possess, and so we don't realize how to connect to God. "Many people experience God, but they don't recognize their own experience," Jesuit Father William Johnston, the author of several books on prayer, stressed. "It's like the two disciples going to Emmaus. They met Jesus on the road but they thought he was a stranger. Only afterwards did they look back and say, 'Were not our hearts burning within us while he was talking to us on the road?'"

Like grace, of course, God's presence is a gift, and we cannot force ourselves into living communion with him by a sheer act of will. Human friendship is similar. We cannot force another man or woman to be our friend or lover. We can only offer our friendship to the other and then humbly await the gift of his or her friendship.

The essence of prayer consists in this humble waiting—in a childlike openness and expectation and listening. To pray means to make ourselves present and available to God so that we are truly ready to open the door when Jesus comes and knocks.

In prayer, we assume an attitude of readiness so that we are alert when God comes to offer his gift. Fortunately, the Good News is that God wants to give us the gift of his presence and his friendship at all times. He is always standing at the door, knocking—always inviting us to be dwelling places of his Spirit.

As Natural as Breathing

Prayer is as natural to us as breathing—or at least it should be. For Christians, both are necessary to life. Prayer is basically personal, and the ways in which we pray reflect our own personal spirituality and belief. It is as unique to each one of us as our fingerprints.

Prayer is a one-to-one relationship with God, a loving Father, as we experience him. It is, in effect, all about my life with him. At the same time, however personal it may be, true Christian prayer has certain basic common strands because it involves a community from which no one is excluded.

In the final analysis only the Spirit of God can teach us how to pray or give us the words to express our needs and deepest spiritual feelings (see Romans 8:26–27). The Spirit prays in and through us, and without the presence of the Spirit we cannot pray, there can be no true Christian prayer. How each individual prays depends on his or her unique situation and present relationship with God and the community. No hard or fast set of rules can be laid down, because we are dealing with matters of the Spirit.

The goal of prayer is conversation with God, to be with God, especially in praise and thanksgiving, but also for petition and intercession.

Just as there should be times spent in talking to God, so should there be times for listening to God in prayer. What he says to us is much more important than what we say to him. Prayer is not a matter of talking a great deal but of loving a great deal. It is thinking about God while loving him, and loving him while thinking about him.

Silence, for the Christian, is not just the absence of speech but also the stillness of soul in which our true self is united with its Creator and Father. We become silent in awe and wonder, as we contemplate God within us. It is an experience too rich and delicate for words.

But because we are human, we use words. Formal prayers may focus on the time of day; any event of our lives; our awareness of God's presence; imploring the help and guidance of the Holy Spirit; a particular need of our world and community; someone who is ill; some spiritual need for ourselves; or, a petition for the assistance of Our Lady, the angels, or the saints.

We may pray using a traditional prayer, such as the Our Father, Hail Mary, or Glory Be; a favorite litany or a phrase from it; a phrase that we repeat over and over, like the Jesus Prayer; a Catholic devotion, such as the Stations of the Cross or the rosary; or spontaneous prayer, which means using our own words to address God. As a sacramental people, we pray as a community through the sacraments, especially and most frequently at Mass.

Prayer When We Are Angry with God

There are times in most, if not all, Christians' lives where feelings of anger or frustration, anguish or annoyance in the face of an evil or uncomfortable, stressful, abandoning, or lonely situations occur. Such times, which we may term as "anger with God," could actually represent the awkward start of a deeper, more honest faith.

It's important to make a clear distinction between the human feeling of anger and the human decision to act hatefully toward another person or God. When the word *anger* is used here, it does not necessarily imply hatred. In the Christian code, of course, it is never moral or Christ-like to act deliberately in a hateful manner toward another human person, much less toward an all-good God.

We recognize, too, that our anger with God is sometimes a bit of a misstatement. Often our anger is really not directed at God, but at the cancer or lightning or human behavior that strikes us, or a loved one, down. The temptation to blame God for these tragedies—or for not averting them—is often based on our incomplete understanding of God and of "God's will," and of how God operates in nature and in human affairs.

Although we don't always think too clearly at times of tragedy, we may need to realize that the anger we first feel toward God should not, in fairness, really be aimed at God but rather at the evil thing or event afflicting us. Keeping these things in mind, here are a few ways we can bring our anger and other honest feelings before God.

1. *Admit your anger if that's what you feel.* Many people wrongly believe that anger must always be destructive—that it is clearly a bad feeling or emotion, and that anger with God is wrong. But every emotion has an important function for us, and gives us important feedback about what is going on inside us.

We need to see that our feelings are one thing, and our behavior in response to them quite another thing. Feeling anger at someone, for example, does not inevitably mean we will murder or harm that person. Anger can be expressed constructively and could lead someone to stop treating us unfairly. An expression of anger could even help bring about reconciliation.

Feeling angry with God, then, is not bad in itself. In fact, our faith can never grow unless we are honest about our feelings. Once we admit we can be angry with God, we become free to see the many ways in which we can express that anger.

2. *Don't restrict yourself to "nice" feelings.* Dividing our feelings into "nice" and "not nice" categories encourages us to deny those feelings we label "not nice." Such a denial, however, severely limits our possibilities of dealing with them. Nice people may say, "don't get angry with God." But what price do they pay for being

nice? Denying honest, healthy feelings reinforces the idea that "not nice" feelings automatically lead to "not nice" behavior.

In the late 1960s, Elisabeth Kübler-Ross discovered that "nice" people who do not want to admit that a friend or relative is dying actually hinder that person from going through the five stages of grief (denial, anger, bargaining, depression, and acceptance). Her book *On Death and Dying* showed that dying persons often have fewer problems in admitting their condition than do friends or relatives who cling to denial in order to protect their own feelings. In the final stages of a terminal illness, in fact, a dying person who has come to acceptance will avoid people whose own need to deny the situation is stronger than the dying person's need to live honestly with it.

Admitting our anger with God does not destroy faith but rather forces us to clarify what we believe and why, to move from a child's faith to an adult's faith. Though refusing to admit anger with God may seem to protect one's faith, in the long run it does more harm than good.

3. *Let your honesty lead to growth in faith.* In 1986, Sister Suzanne Schrautemyer went to a doctor because of a lump under her left arm. Tests showed that cancer had spread to her bone marrow. Earlier, she had undergone a partial mastectomy, a bilateral mastectomy, radiation treatment, and chemotherapy. At this point, Sr. Suzanne (at the time age thirty-nine) decided to accept her coming death and discontinue chemotherapy.

She went through several months of low-grade anger and depression, having difficulty talking about it with anyone. "I had to be assured it's okay to be angry, to doubt, to be broken and down," she said. "I don't believe now that my faith is insulted by my anger and doubt. I had to move through it—those real human experiences—before I could let go of it."

Did her faith change during that ordeal? "Yes, it's simpler," she told a newspaper reporter. "I used to think some places, people, times were more sacred than others. My experience of faith now tells me that everything, every moment is sacred. Everything that happens is a sacrament, a moment when God becomes tangible and life is real. That's what's different."

Admitting her anger did not cure Sr. Suzanne of her cancer, but it allowed her to live honestly, to choose how she would deal with her feelings rather than try to pretend they didn't exist. Such honesty led her to a more adult faith, to a fuller appreciation of the present moment and of God's providence. Thus, her initial anger with God led not to denying her faith or going through the motions but to a deeper, richer faith able to put its arms around all of life—even her coming death.

4. *Be careful how you speak of "God's will."* In dealing with tragedies many people, including religious men and women, often describe them as "God's will." Unfortunately, people who readily speak of "God's will" in such circumstances are frequently the same people who acknowledge only their "nice" feelings.

People who refuse to admit any anger with God and who immediately describe a tragedy as God's will may have the best of intentions. Experience, however, shows us that people most often speak about suffering as God's will when they are talking about someone else's suffering. We can describe any suffering as God's will in the sense that God has not intervened to prevent that suffering from striking some individual. Or God "allows" the laws of nature to follow their normal course.

Doesn't it make more sense to describe God's will as what we know God wants—that each person share in the divine life and reflect the image of God in which he or she was created? God wants people to be healthy and fully alive. Glib talk about God's will for other people can easily excuse us from seeing, offering, and experiencing the works of compassion and mercy which Jesus praised.

5. *Express your feelings honestly when you pray.* Because most people think that prayer should always be a peaceful, serene experience, they have trouble imagining that an angry person could really pray—better to wait until he or she has cooled down before praying.

Unfortunately, grieving people who accept that message frequently try to pray (communicate with God) without ever mentioning the most important things or feelings that need to be communicated. Such an attitude leads either to superficial prayers (being nice at all costs) or abandoning prayer as dishonest. People who pray honestly in anger can grow into a faith that is perhaps not as "nice" as before but is obviously more honest. Moreover, these are the people who are most ready to understand and assist others who are bandaging up life's physical or emotional wounds.

Praying amid my own anger or encouraging someone else to pray honestly in his or her anger may feel awkward and not much like any prayer I've ever known. From such soil, however, God may nurture a faith unlike the one I had—or the other person had—when everything went very smoothly and there was no reason to pray in anger.

6. *Recognize when it's time to move beyond anger*. Admitting the anger does not entitle us to special handling for the rest of our lives. People frozen in anger can become as callous as people who prefer being nice at all costs. Dealing with anger—our own or someone else's—can lead to growth, to deeper compassion, to a deeper faith in God. Dealing with anger will not erase sorrow, but it will enable a person to live honestly and to help others who have experienced great loss. If anger becomes a permanent condition, however, the person stops long before the journey is complete.

Our goal is an adult faith in God—however much that may resemble or differ from the faith in God we had as children.

Adults ready to grow in faith can face their anger, recognize their God-given freedom in the face of it, and encourage others to do the same.

Questions for Reflection

1. What forms of prayer do you feel most comfortable with?
2. How do you block distractions when you pray?
3. Have you ever been angry with God? When? How did you express that anger? If you did not express that anger in prayer, why?

CHAPTER TWO

The Mass: Our Communal Prayer Form

How many of the things that you did when you were ten years old do you still do today? This is especially true of physical activities, but it can encompass seemingly every aspect of life. That includes the possibility that our own prayer lives can change.

Most likely, there are some prayers and devotions we may have prayed in our youth that we no longer pray. The Mass, however, remains constant in our lives and in the life of the Church. After two thousand years, God's invitation to the banquet still stands.

There are specific reasons why we go to Mass and why it has become such a foundational element in the prayer lives of Catholics around the world.

1. *We need others to pray well.* It is hard to do difficult things alone, and following Jesus can be tough work. One of the reasons why Alcoholics Anonymous and other twelve-step programs, Weight Watchers, and other similar organizations work is because they are group efforts. To change our lives in biblical terms, to repent, to convert, we need the help and support of others.

At Mass, we are reminded and assured that we are not alone in our efforts. We are members of the Church. We are members of the Body of Christ. We share in the Spirit of Christ and we are empowered by that Holy Spirit.

At each Eucharist, we hear the words: "For this is the chalice of my blood, the blood of the new and eternal covenant, which will be poured out for you and for many for the forgiveness of sins." Together we can make a difference in this world. Together with Christ we can make a tremendous difference. And at Mass, we are truly gathered with Christ: "For where two or three are gathered in my name, I am there among them" (Matthew 18:20).

2. *The Mass enables me to pray with my whole body.* When we pray by ourselves, at home, we usually pray with words, talking to God. But when we attend Mass, we pray with more than words; we pray with our whole bodies. Our prayer at Mass includes bread and wine, water and oil, coming together and going apart, standing still and processing forward, lighting candles and smelling flowers, even dust and ashes on our foreheads!

At Mass, we acknowledge that each of us is more than just mind or soul, but rather saved body and soul, saved body, mind, and spirit. We are saved by a God who is more than just spirit. We are saved by a God who "became flesh and lived among us" (John 1:14). Because of the Incarnation, we can approach God not only with words, but also with the elements of our daily lives, eating and drinking, sharing meals, and singing songs.

The beauty of the Mass is that it becomes an experience beyond description. It means more than we can ever understand it to mean, more than just words. At Mass, we pray with our whole selves, body, mind, and spirit.

3. *Besides talking to God, I need God to talk to me.* We too often think of prayer only as talking to God. A real conversation, however, needs not only talking but also listening. At Mass, we have the opportunity to listen to God speaking to each of us.

It is Christ's voice we hear in the readings, since it is he himself who speaks when the holy Scriptures are read in the Church (Constitution on the Sacred Liturgy, 7). We can hear Christ's voice in the homily. We can hear his voice in the other members of the worshiping assembly in their devotion, their petitions, and their sacrifices. And, most especially, we hear his voice in the prayers of the Mass.

At each Mass we hear Christ's words: "This is my body which will be given up for you." God speaks to us in these words, and we hear proclaimed the reality of the central mystery of faith: Christ died for our sins, rose from the dead, and gives us his body and blood to eat and drink.

When we hear the words "Do this in memory of me," we hear God's voice not just challenging us to go to Mass but also challenging us directly to that self-giving love that the Mass celebrates. We are to become the Body of Christ, to live as Christ lived and act as Christ would act.

4. *Being born again once didn't quite do it.* We know that baptism is a new birth and that in baptism all of our sins are taken away. But we continue to sin and we continue to need to hear the words, "Your sins are forgiven."

When we participate at Mass, we are continually assured of God's ongoing love. Consider how many times during Mass we seek God's mercy: "May almighty God...forgive us our sins" (Penitential Rite); "You take away the sins of the world, have mercy on us" (Glory to God); "To us, also, your servants, who, though sinners, hope in your abundant mercies...not weighing our merits, but granting us your pardon, through Christ our Lord" (Eucharistic Prayer I); "Our Father...forgive us our trespasses as we forgive those who trespass against us" (Lord's Prayer); "Behold the Lamb of God, behold him who takes away the sins of the world.... Lord, I am not worthy...but only say the word and my soul shall be healed" (Invitation to Communion).

While we were born again through the sacrament of baptism, we need to be born again, and again, and again. We promise again, as we promised or our parents and godparents promised for us at baptism, to die to sin and to reject Satan, and all his works and all his empty promises. At each Mass, we promise again to follow more closely in the footsteps of Jesus.

Each time we enter the church for Mass, we sign ourselves with water from the baptismal font, or holy water font, as a reminder of our baptism. Mass is a way to renew and repeat over and over the promises of our baptism.

Questions for Reflection

1. Why do you go to Mass on Sunday? What would you miss most if you did not go?
2. What helps you feel connected to God at Mass? To the others with whom you are celebrating Mass?
3. How does the Mass help you affirm your baptism?

CHAPTER THREE

Foundations of Our Faith: The Creed and the Our Father

The Apostles' Creed

I believe in God,

the Father almighty,

Creator of heaven and earth,

and in Jesus Christ, his only Son, our Lord,

who was conceived by the Holy Spirit,

born of the Virgin Mary,

suffered under Pontius Pilate,

was crucified, died and was buried;

he descended into hell;

on the third day he rose again from the dead;

he ascended into heaven,

and is seated at the right hand of God the Father almighty;

from there he will come to judge the living and the dead.
I believe in the Holy Spirit,
the holy catholic Church,
the communion of saints,
the forgiveness of sins,
the resurrection of the body,
and life everlasting.
Amen.

The Nicene Creed

I believe in one God,
the Father almighty,
maker of heaven and earth,
of all things visible and invisible.
I believe in one Lord Jesus Christ,
the Only Begotten Son of God,
born of the Father before all ages.
God from God, Light from Light,
true God from true God,
begotten, not made, consubstantial with the Father;
through him all things were made.
For us men and for our salvation
he came down from heaven,
and by the Holy Spirit was incarnate of the Virgin Mary,
and became man.

For our sake he was crucified under Pontius Pilate,
he suffered death and was buried,
and rose again on the third day
in accordance with the Scriptures.
He ascended into heaven
and is seated at the right hand of the Father.
He will come again in glory
to judge the living and the dead
and his kingdom will have no end.
I believe in the Holy Spirit, the Lord, the giver of life,
who proceeds from the Father and the Son,
who with the Father and the Son is adored and glorified,
who has spoken through the prophets.
I believe in one, holy, catholic and apostolic Church.
I confess one Baptism for the forgiveness of sins
and I look forward to the resurrection of the dead
and the life of the world to come. Amen.

A creed is an authoritative summary of Christianity's basic beliefs. In the articles of the Creed, we profess our faith in mysteries— doctrines that could never be known apart from divine revelation. If God had not revealed the mysteries of Christianity, the mysteries we speak in the Creed, we could never have figured them out on our own.

A creed is not the totality of Christian faith. It's a summary that stands for everything that is taught by the Catholic Church, which is itself one of the mysteries we proclaim in the Creed. A creed is a symbol of something larger—and, ultimately, of Someone we love, Someone who loves us and makes us who we are, by means of creeds and other graces.

The *Catechism of the Catholic Church* puts it eloquently when it says that our faith does not rest ultimately in formulas, but in the realities expressed by those formulas, which faith allows us to touch (see *CCC*, 170). Faith is our personal clinging to God and to his truth in its entirety (see *CCC*, 150). Yet we cannot love someone whom we do not know. The propositions of the Creed help us along the way of knowledge.

The Need for a Creed

The word *creed* comes from the Latin word *credo*—literally translated: "I believe!"—which is the phrase with which Christians have always begun their profession. There is strong evidence that such summary acts of faith have been integral to Christianity from the very start.

Credo (or its Aramaic equivalent) is the word cried out by the desperate father who begs Jesus for the healing of his child (see Mark 9:24). St. Paul seems to allude to creedal statements when he says: "if you confess with your lips that Jesus is Lord and believe in your heart that God raised him from the dead, you will be saved. For one believes with the heart and so is justified, and one confesses with the mouth and so is saved" (Romans 10:9–10).

A creed marks the way of conversion, for a pilgrim Church on earth and for each of its members to say what we mean, and mean what we say as we walk the talk.

Creeds have always been an important part of the Rite of Baptism. This was one way the early Church made sure to fulfill Jesus's command: "Go therefore and make disciples of all nations, baptizing them in the name of the Father and of the Son and of the Holy Spirit" (Matthew 28:19). Some of the most ancient creeds we know are simple statements professing belief in each of the persons of the blessed Trinity. If they elaborate at all, they add statements affirming that Jesus is both God and man.

From early on, there were two general types of creeds: the question-and-answer kind and the declaration kind. We still know both forms today.

The Church uses the question-and-answer form in baptism and at the Easter Vigil. It expresses the movement of conversion in dramatic terms as it moves from a rejection of sin and evil ("Do you reject Satan?" "I do.") to an affirmation of the true God ("Do you believe in God the Father Almighty…?" "I do").

Each "I do" resounds with power, glory, and strength of commitment, reminding us of marriage vows and solemn oaths sworn in courtrooms. Like marriage, the Creed indeed changes us. It marks a key moment in the story of our ongoing conversion.

But the "declaration creed" is even more familiar to us. We recite one of them at every Sunday Mass, and they are made up of a series of sentences that declare our belief in many distinct (but interrelated) mysteries: God's fatherhood, Jesus's divine sonship, the Holy Spirit's divinity, the Church's mission, future judgment and life everlasting.

The revised *Roman Missal* gives us both the Nicene Creed and the Apostles' Creed. The Nicene Creed is based upon the faith expressed at the first two ecumenical councils of the Church: the fourth-century Councils of Nicaea (325) and Constantinople (381). The Apostles' Creed is significantly shorter and less detailed; it is based upon the most ancient formula used by the Church in Rome; we find it in various forms dating back to the 200s.

The Creed, as it has come down to us, conveys the relational core of Christian faith. In telling the truth about the Father, Son, and Holy Spirit, we profess that the mystery of God is the interpersonal relations we are called to share. We proclaim the relationship for which we have been reborn, and by which we are empowered to live as Jesus lived, to die with Jesus, and to rise again to everlasting life.

And so, in the words of the Church, we "renew" our baptism with the words of the Creed. And we are renewed. We are made a new creation, "being transformed into the same image" (2 Corinthians 3:18).

The Our Father

Our Father, who art in heaven,

hallowed be thy name;

thy kingdom come;

thy will be done on earth as it is in heaven.

Give us this day our daily bread;

and forgive us our trespasses

as we forgive those who trespass

against us;

and lead us not into temptation,

but deliver us from evil.

Amen.

The words of the Our Father are signposts to interior prayer. They provide a basic direction for our being, and they aim to configure us to the image of the Son. The meaning of the Our Father goes much further than the mere provision of a prayer text. It aims to form our being, to train us in the inner attitude of Jesus (see Philippians 2:5).

When the disciples were unsure about how to express their new and more intimate relationship with God, they appointed one of their number to ask for directions. He approached Jesus at prayer and said, "Lord, teach us to pray." Jesus responded, "When you pray, say: 'Father, hallowed be your name...'" (Luke 11:1–2).

The prayer Jesus gave his friends was as good as a map into the kingdom of God. "You may look through all the prayers in the

Scriptures," St. Augustine said, "but you will not find anything that is not contained in the Lord's Prayer."

Recognizing the Our Father as the Lord's gift to his faith community, the Church has always prayed it daily. No celebration of baptism, confirmation, or Eucharist, no offering of the Liturgy of the Hours is complete without this universal prayer. We know the words so well we could recite them in our sleep. Therein is the danger that we may pray them like a sleepwalker making nightly rounds.

"Our Father …"
Who is this first Person of the Trinity whom Jesus calls "Father"? Only the Son knows the answer: "Whoever has seen me has seen the Father" (John 14:9). But when we pray to the Father, we "enter into his mystery as he is and as the Son has revealed him to us" (*Catechism of the Catholic Church*, 2779). This much we do know: The Father is more than our paternal image of him. Human language and images, after all, are inadequate to express the reality of God.

The *Catechism* makes the reassuring point that the word *our* excludes no one. If we are sincere in using that communal pronoun, "our divisions and oppositions have to be overcome" (2792). We cannot pray "our" without including every single person for whom Christ died. The Our Father erases all boundaries between us and them, between past and present.

The *our* of the Our Father calls us into the family circle, saints rubbing elbows with sinners, rich with poor, criminal with law-abiding, powerful with victimized, beloved with despised, living with dead. There are no outcasts from the "our."

"Hallowed be thy name…"
The Lord's Prayer respects the priority of praise over petitions in our own behalf. "It is characteristic of love to think first of the one whom we love" (*Catechism of the Catholic Church*, 2804). Therefore, the first three affirmations of the Our Father bear the aroma of selflessness as we say: We love you, we hallow your name, we desire your kingdom and the fulfillment of your will.

"Thy kingdom come…"
We recognize that the kingdom has come in Christ himself and will come in glory when Jesus appears at the end time. Sometimes, in the midst of a Eucharist celebration, we actually sense that the kingdom is, as Jesus said, right at hand.

What we pray for we must be willing to work for insofar as we are able. The kingdom parables of Jesus show that the disciples must exert effort. The sower must harvest both weeds and wheat; the mustard seed requires a sower. The yeast cannot leaven the loaf unless it is kneaded. The treasure in the field and the pearl of great price must be sought and purchased at considerable sacrifice. The net cannot cast itself, nor the haul be separated without the fisherman.

"Thy will be done, on earth as it is in heaven…"

This beautiful petition unites us with Jesus, who says, "My food is to do the will of him who sent me" (John 4:34), and with Mary who responds to God's call with "let it be with me according to your word" (Luke 1:38). To desire and to do God's will is our highest purpose.

"Give us this day our daily bread…"

The One who taught us to pray these words assures us that if we ask, we will receive (see Matthew 7:7–11).

What is the bread we seek? It is the Bread of Life itself in Eucharist. It is food on the table and hospitality to a guest. It is "all appropriate goods and blessings, both material and spiritual" (*CCC*, 2830). And what we ask for we must be willing to give insofar as we are able. We cannot hope to receive a hearty loaf of seven-grain bread if we are giving no more than a loaf-shaped stone to those who hunger for three square meals a day, for companionship, for work, for the Word of God.

"Forgive us our trespasses, as we forgive those who trespass against us…"

Here, we know not what we pray! Who among us has not met at least one impossible-to-forgive person? What a joy it must be to learn to forgive like the father of the prodigal son!

"While he was still far off," Luke says, "his father saw him and was filled with compassion; he ran and put his arms around him and kissed him" (Luke 15:20). How liberating for the father as well as for the son! To forgive others as the Father has forgiven us is a life's work worthy of the best we have to give.

"And lead us not into temptation…"
This awkward translation from the Greek seems to cast God the Father as a sly trickster who on occasion dangles forbidden fruit before our noses just to see what we will do. But, as Pope Benedict has said, "God certainly does not lead us into temptation." He points to St. James, who tells us, "No one, when tempted, should say, 'I am being tempted by God'; for God cannot be tempted by evil and he himself tempts no one" (James 1:13).

What we are really asking our loving Father for is the gift of discernment: "Do not allow us to enter into temptation" and "do not let us yield to temptation" (*CCC*, 2846). As many of the saints have noted, temptation itself is good for us. Without it, we would be untried warriors who, in our first major battle against evil, wind up as casualties or prisoners to sin.

"But deliver us from evil…"
The Church recognizes Satan as the "ruler of this world" (John 14:30), "the father of lies," "the angel who opposes God" and "throws himself across God's plan and his work of salvation accomplished in Christ" (*CCC*, 2851–2852).

How do we recognize this arch-deceiver, this unholy adversary, this thorn in our collective side? We will know him by his bulging sack of glossy possessions, vain ambitions, useless fears, and seductive control buttons. He works under cover of darkness and the fruit of his labors is discord. He sets husband against wife, parent against child, black against white, nation against nation, one faith against another.

We oppose Satan best by sticking together, closing ranks around God, our caring Father. "Resist the devil," St. James advises, "and he will flee from you" (4:7).

In his 2007 book, *Jesus of Nazareth*, Pope Benedict said the Our Father is "trying to tell us that it is only when you have lost God that you have lost yourself; then you are nothing more than a random product of evolution. This, then, is why we pray from the depths of our soul not to be robbed of our faith, which enables us to see God, which binds us with Christ."

Questions for Reflection

1. How does saying the Creed, whether at Mass or on your own, help in your understanding the Catholic faith?

2. What part of the Our Father speaks most strongly to you, and why?

3. Do these traditional prayers inspire you to pray in non-traditional ways?

CHAPTER FOUR

Other Forms of Prayer

There are many prayer paths available to us today. Each of us must find the styles of prayer that suit us. The Holy Spirit is the only true teacher of prayer, and without preconceived ideas, we must let the Spirit draw us to those ways of prayer that best work for us.

Any good spiritual director will warn you against methods of prayer that do not harmonize with your spiritual gifts. With this in mind, let's explore the following approaches to prayer, some of which—if adapted to your needs—can lead to a richer union with God.

Praying with the Bible

If you are like many people, the Bible is at once an old friend and a stranger. You recognize it easily, as you would an old friend, and trust it as a companion. You know that it contains a record of

God's sacred Word to humanity. You take comfort in knowing that you can pick it up at any time and find something in it of value.

But for many Catholics, the only time they experience Scripture is during the recitation of Old and New Testament readings during daily or weekly Mass. As a result, reading and praying the Bible can be intimidating. Here are some tips for reading and praying the Bible outside of Mass:

Don't begin at the beginning or end. Begin with the familiar. For Christians, the New Testament is a better place to start than the Old Testament. Perhaps begin with Mark, the shortest Gospel, or the letters of Paul. Do not start with the book of Revelation, a complex and symbolic book.

Read aloud. Everyone used to do it, especially when the books of the Bible were written. The Bible was meant to be heard—it originated as an oral tradition. Reading aloud involves you more completely than reading silently.

Invoke the Holy Spirit. Every time you sit down to pray with the Bible begin with a brief prayer to call upon the guidance of the Holy Spirit. Something as simple as "Come, Holy Spirit, be my guide as I try to understand this Word" reminds us that we need to surrender to God in order to understand the Word properly.

Choose a passage to reflect on. Working through the whole book of the Bible prayerfully is more effective than random interpretations. Another way of doing this is to pray along with the lectionary selections for the upcoming Sunday Mass. That can help you prepare to hear the Word more fruitfully when it is proclaimed and preached upon the following Sunday. In three years' time, you'll have prayed along with most of the Bible!

Read the passage once through fully. Getting the big picture first helps you understand each section or passage better.

Read each section of the passage slowly. Slow, meditative reading is an ancient Christian practice known as lectio divina (see the next section). Sitting with the text, mulling over its words and phrases and soaking in its images or themes, truly brings one to a prayerful understanding. Let the words sink in, and you will feel yourself in the presence of God.

Use your imagination. Although this approach may not work for every passage, it can be very prayerful for some. Imagine yourself in the text. Where are you? Are there characters with whom you identify? Do you see yourself in any actions?

Reread the entire passage. Once you have spent time reflecting on some sections of a passage, reread it in its entirety. Though some parts may have spoken to you more clearly, this exercise will help you remember to keep the section in context.

Conclude with a prayer of thanksgiving. Thank God for the gift of the Word as you conclude your prayer exercise. It is God's Word that gives us life.

Lectio Divina

Lectio divina, a Latin term meaning "divine reading," is a practice of slow, contemplative praying of the Scriptures through which we open ourselves to God speaking to us through his Word, and discover the ability to be more embracing of our relationship to the Trinity. This can be done either alone or in a group.

It has its roots in traditional Benedictine practice of scriptural reading, meditation, and prayer dating back to the sixth century, established by St. Benedict. It is generally recognized that Carthusian monk Guigo II formalized the practice in the twelfth century.

In 1965, the Second Vatican Council emphasized the use of *lectio divina* in its dogmatic constitution *Dei Verbum* (Word of God). On the fortieth anniversary of *Dei Verbum* in 2005 Pope Benedict XVI reaffirmed its importance:

> I would like in particular to recall and recommend the ancient tradition of lectio divina: the diligent reading of Sacred Scripture accompanied by prayer brings about that intimate dialogue in which the person reading hears God who is speaking, and in praying, responds to him with trusting openness of heart (cf. *Dei Verbum,* n. 25). If it is effectively promoted, this practice will bring to the Church—I am convinced of it—a new spiritual springtime.

Traditionally, *lectio divina* has four separate steps: read, meditate, pray, and contemplate. A Scripture passage is read, and then its meaning is reflected upon. Prayer and then contemplation follow. What it is not is a theological analysis or an analytical approach to or study of the Bible; rather, *lectio divina* is a way whereby the practitioner can enter into a more peaceful place to share Christ's peace in our own lives.

The first stage is *lectio*, a slow, reflective, attentive reading of the Word of God, which might include rereading several times so that it sinks into us. Any passage of Scripture can be used for this way of prayer but the passage should not be too long.

The second stage—*meditatio*—offers a chance for reflection where we think about the text we have chosen and reflect on the message of the Scripture that God is communicating to us. The key here is to remain open to the interpretation guided by the Holy Spirit rather than by analysis of the text and our placing our own meaning on it.

Oratio, or response to God (prayer) follows, where we set our thinking aside and simply let our hearts speak to God. Our prayer of petition, thanksgiving, adoration, praise, repentance, or any other response is inspired by our reflection on the Word of God.

The final stage of *lectio divina* is *contemplatio* or contemplation, silent prayers that "are not speeches; they are like kindling that feeds the fire of love" and represent "a union with the prayer of

Christ" (CCC, 2717–2718). It is here in silence that we rest in the Word of God, listen at the core of our being to God who speaks within us, and where we are gradually transformed from within.

The Way of the Cross

The Stations of the Cross are a series of artistic representations depicting those final hours of Jesus before he died and the devotions that commemorate the Passion. It is also known as the Way of the Cross (in Latin, *Via Crucis*) or the Way of Sorrows (*Via Dolorosa*) of that path that Jesus walked to Calvary.

St. Francis of Assisi is credited with beginning the tradition of trying to offer to the faithful a way to actually walk in prayer in the steps of Jesus on those final hours of what we now observe as Good Friday. Most Roman Catholic churches now contain representations of the stations—small plaques, paintings, or other artistic depictions—typically placed at intervals along the side walls of its naves. While most Stations of the Cross contain fourteen stations, some series contain a fifteenth station representing the Resurrection, as a completion of the journey that began at the garden of Gethsemane.

In approaching each of the stations, there should be a sense of adoration and praise followed by the naming of the station, an opening prayer, a reflection on that station in the life of Jesus and how it relates to our own lives, and a closing prayer. A verse of the *Stabat Mater* (At the Cross Her Station Keeping) or other appropriate antiphon is often sung while moving to the next station.

The Stations of the Cross are:

First Station: Jesus is condemned to death.

Second Station: Jesus accepts his cross.

Third Station: Jesus falls the first time.

Fourth Station: Jesus meets his sorrowful mother.

Fifth Station: Simon helps Jesus carry the cross.

Sixth Station: Veronica wipes the face of Jesus.

Seventh Station: Jesus falls for the second time.

Eighth Station: Jesus speaks to the weeping woman.

Ninth Station: Jesus falls for the third time.

Tenth Station: Jesus is stripped of his garments.

Eleventh Station: Jesus is nailed to the cross.

Twelfth Station: Jesus dies on the cross.

Thirteenth Station: Jesus is taken down from the cross.

Fourteenth Station: Jesus is laid in the tomb.

The Stations of the Cross offer the Christian an opportunity to be led by Jesus into the presence of God. The Way allows us to symbolically walk with Jesus on his journey to the cross, and reinforce our commitment to follow him in loving service to humanity.

The Rosary

The words of the rosary are meant to launch us into the mysteries of Christ's life or, better, into the living mystery of Christ himself, who says, "I am with you always even until the end of time." Just as each Hail Mary builds up to the word Jesus, so the whole rosary leads to union with him. And through Jesus we come into union with the Triune God.

Each decade ends with "Glory be to Father, to the Son, and to the Holy Spirit..." suggesting that the whole rosary is a movement toward praise and joyful union with God.

In praying the rosary, it's important not to get too tied down or worried about the words, at least, not to get anxious about them. If you feel inspired to savor the words and their meaning, that's fine. There is a scriptural richness and a spiritual energy to be tapped from the words themselves.

Most important is to pray from the heart. Many people who say the rosary consider the words to be like background music leading them more deeply into the mysteries or into God's loving presence within. The gentle murmur of the words, for example can take us into that silent center within us where Jesus' Spirit dwells as in a temple.

How to Pray the Rosary

The Joyful Mysteries (usually prayed on Mondays and Saturdays)

1. The Annunciation to Mary that She Is to Be the Mother of the Savior (Luke 1:26–38).
2. The Visitation of Mary to Her Cousin Elizabeth (Luke 1:39–47).
3. The Nativity of Our Lord Jesus Christ (Luke 2:1–7).

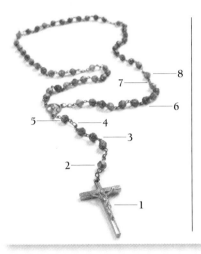

1. Make the Sign of the Cross and pray the Apostles' Creed.
2. Pray the Our Father.
3. Pray three Hail Marys.
4. Pray the Glory Be.
5. Announce the mystery for reflection and pray the Our Father.
6. Pray 10 Hail Marys.
7. Finish the decade with the Glory Be.
8. Repeat this process (5,6,7) for each decade.

4. The Presentation of the Infant Jesus in the Temple (Luke 2:22–32).
5. The Finding of the Child Jesus in the Temple (Luke 2:41–52).

The Luminous Mysteries (usually prayed on Thursdays)

1. The Baptism of Jesus in the Jordan (Matthew 3:17).
2. The Wedding Feast at Cana (John 2:1– 12).
3. The Proclamation of the Kingdom of God/The Call to Conversion (Mark 1:15; Mark 2:3–13; Luke 7:47–48; John 20:22–23).
4. The Transfiguration (Luke 9:35).
5. The First Eucharist (John 13:1).

The Sorrowful Mysteries (usually prayed on Tuesdays and Fridays)

1. The Agony of Christ in the Garden (Mark 14:32–36).
2. The Scourging of Jesus at the Pillar (John 18:28–38; 19:1).
3. The Crowning with Thorns (Mark 15:16–20).
4. The Carrying of the Cross (John 19:12–16).
5. The Crucifixion and Death of Jesus (Luke 23:33–34, 39–46).

The Glorious Mysteries (usually prayed on Sundays and Wednesdays)

1. The Resurrection of Jesus (Luke 24:1–6).
2. The Ascension of Our Lord into Heaven (Luke 24:50–53).
3. The Descent of the Holy Spirit (Acts 2:1–4).
4. The Assumption of Mary into Heaven (Song of Songs 2:8–14).
5. The Coronation of Our Lady in Heaven (Revelation 12:1–6).

The Hail Mary

Hail Mary, full of grace, the Lord is with you;

blessed are you among women,

and blessed is the fruit of your womb, Jesus.

Holy Mary, Mother of God,

pray for us sinners

now and at the hour of our death.

Amen.

The Glory Be

Glory be to the Father, the Son, and the Holy Spirit;
as it was in the beginning, is now, and ever shall be,
world without end.
Amen.

Centering Prayer

Centering prayer is a method of silent prayer that directs the participant to still the flow of thoughts and desires that keep the mind and heart constantly occupied. In doing so, we can become more fully available to experience the presence of God and develop a deeper, closer relationship with the Father, the living Christ, and the Holy Spirit.

Many shy away from the idea of meditation or contemplation, believing that it is only for special people or those deeply spiritual or religious. In reality, everyone meditates, but the subject of meditation differs. Those who desire to be Olympic athletes literally think, eat, and sleep their sports. Persons who believe that money is the source of happiness also meditate daily, as thoughts about making and investing money constantly absorb their minds. For spiritual seekers, the divine mystery is the subject of contemplation.

While God is present to all things, God is also beyond anything we can put our fingers on. Moreover, God cannot be contained by our concepts and thoughts. In silent prayer or the prayer of contemplation, the pilgrim seeks to still the endless river of thoughts so as to find the center from which all thoughts arise, the center within which peace and God reside.

The following exercises can help us take those steps on that essential journey inward:

Sit still and quiet the body. The first requirement for any journey inward is to quiet the body, which so easily absorbs the countless energies of life that surround it. Without straining, sit with your head, neck, and back erect. For a few moments, simply notice what's happening in your body without trying to change it. Be aware of where you are stiff or tense. Then, without slouching, let your body be supported by the floor or the chair; let it become quiet.

Gently begin to breathe deeply. As you breathe, be conscious of the act of breathing that you normally take for granted. At first, simply notice your breath without any attempt to control it. Then gently let the breath become fuller and deeper. Do not strain, but let your breathing be slow, even, and deep.

Let yourself rest in peace. Sitting in stillness, allow yourself to be absorbed in peace and into God's presence. To help quiet your mind, use a single word or phrase that is repeated over and over with great devotion. The word can be a name of God (Jesus, Abba, Lord), a phrase from a psalm or other book of Scripture, or a word of great power like "love" or "peace."

Go inward, silently repeating your sacred word or phrase. Let your mind rest solely upon your sacred word or phrase. Invest it with as much devotion as possible. Inevitably, a thought or idea will rise up into your mind. Do not resist it or attempt to expel it and avoid judging yourself. Instead of trying to push it away, quietly and with great devotion simply turn your attention back to your sacred word.

Be at peace in God. What we seek in prayer cannot be achieved by sheer force of will, by laboring, or by forcing the mind to concentrate. The purpose of meditation is to be absorbed in God. As a sponge absorbs water, so our minds should be absorbed by the sound of the sacred word and, beyond that, absorbed in God's presence. Let yourself rest peacefully in God.

Examen of Consciousness

St. Ignatius Loyola, founder of the Society of Jesus, recommended to his Jesuit brothers a daily method of examining their lives so that they might better serve the Lord. Ignatius proposed a daily exercise, which he called the Examen, that has been used by many Christians ever since. Through this daily practice, they learn to discern God's will and grow in the understanding of God's beautiful creation.

Now called the Examen of Consciousness, it is not the same as an examination of conscience, such as you engage in before meeting Jesus in the sacrament of reconciliation. The Examen is a methodical prayer that helps you meet Jesus in your daily life, as he encourages you to do God's will.

There are five simple steps to the Examen, which should take about fifteen minutes to complete. It is often best, especially in the evening, to have a special place where you meet God. Then sit comfortably, as straight-backed as possible with both feet on the floor. Feel God's presence and know his deep love for you.

Recall you are in the presence of God. We are always in the presence of God, but in prayer we place ourselves in God's presence in an especially attentive way.

Look at your day with gratitude. After a few moments, begin to give thanks to God for the gifts of this day. As you move in gratitude through the details of your day, remember that every single event has been God's gift. After you review the special gifts of God this day, recall the gifts of your own creation. As you complete the review of your gifts and the particular gifts of this day, pause briefly to thank God for all these.

Ask help from the Holy Spirit. Ask here in a special way for the Holy Spirit to come into your heart and to help you look at your actions this day clearly and with an understanding of your own limitations. The Spirit will help you understand the mystery of your human heart, and at this point you ask to learn more about your actions and motivations. This is not a "beat up on yourself" session; rather, it is a gentle look at how you have responded to God's gifts.

Review your day. Replay the day in your mind, noticing the details, the context of what happened, how you acted, and your interior motives and feelings. Some questions worth asking might be: When and why did I fail? When did I love? What have become my habits and life patterns? Do they bring me closer to God, or keep me away? Where has God acted in my day? The daily Examen will help you to become more sensitive to signs of God's grace in your life and the ways in which Christ influences you: through God's people, the Body of Christ, and through his Word in Scripture.

Reconcile and resolve. The final step is our heart-to-heart talk with Jesus. Imagine him, your trusted friend, sitting right there beside you, or before you. Maybe there was something you did wrong—not particularly sinful, but not particularly smart either. Now is the time to tell Jesus you are sorry, and to ask him to be with you the next time the same sort of situation arises. Remember all of the good things, and thank the Lord for being with you when you avoided a wrong choice, or when you resisted an old temptation. Feel the sorrow in your heart when you apologize, but also feel the gratitude when you give thanks for God's gentle work inside your heart as he continually labors to make you more Christ-like.

End the entire Examen with the Our Father.

Praydreaming: A Tool for Discernment

There are a number of approaches to discernment in the Catholic tradition. St. Ignatius saw that "Good discernment consists of prayerfully pondering the great desires that well up in my daydreams."

Are desires good or bad? Many spiritual writers of Ignatius' day spoke of desires as obstacles to God's will. One solution was to suppress desires—to eliminate them whenever possible. Ignatius saw that not only are desires not evil, but they are one of God's primary instruments of communicating his will to his children. He did not seek to squash desires, but rather sought to tap into the deepest desires of the heart, trusting that it is God who has placed them there.

Desires, of course, play a role in sinful choices, too. But Ignatius would define sin as disordered desire. The problem is not having desires, but that they are disordered within us. That is why we must tap into the greatest, most universal desire among humans: to praise, reverence, and serve God.

We fall into sin when we are ignorant of the desires beneath the desires. Consider this way of understanding personal sin: We sin, not because we are in touch with our desires but precisely because we are not in touch with them! This is one of Ignatius' most profound insights.

How, then, to tap into these great desires? Daydream, that's how! Fantasize about great and beautiful futures. Let God dream in us and sit in silent awe and wonder as these holy dreams come to life before the eyes and ears of our souls.

Note the difference between the way most people normally decide and this radical way of discerning that Ignatius is proposing. Most lead with the wrong foot: They allow the tools of the false spirit to drive us: fear and anxiety ("What will happen?"), ambition, pride, jealousy, and so on. There will be time enough to deal with negative realities. But first we need to allow great desires to lead us. Imagine the greatest potentialities —the best-case scenarios—for each option.

After feeling the initial excitement of new possibilities in your dreams, begin to ponder their meaning and try to note the stirrings in the heart.

Which dreams leave you with a feeling of peace and well-being, oneness with God—what Ignatius would refer to as "consolation"?

Which dreams leave you with a feeling of deep-down anxiety and fear, a sense of distance from God, with no passion and with a sense of boredom or frustration—which Ignatius would call "desolation"?

As you pay attention to these praydreams, note the fluctuating moments of peace vs. disquiet, and of impassioned energy vs. deflatedness.

Ignatius says that when a well-intentioned, prayerful person is in sync with God, God's will comes "sweetly, lightly, gently, as a drop of water that enters a sponge." This inner peace—even for a tough decision—is one of the most important telltale signs of God's will. When pondering praydreams, which of the options leave us feeling a sense of deep-down peace, as opposed to agitation or even simply feeling comfortable with the option?

Often, after many hours of prayerful deliberation, there will be a moment when we will just know. It will feel not as though making a decision but, rather, as though we are acknowledging a decision that has already been agreed upon by God and our hearts.

Once reaching a point of decision, Ignatius suggests we place that decision before God and await his confirmation. How will this confirmation come? In the same way that our initial discernment came. It will be through pondering the stirrings of our hearts as we begin to take the first tentative steps toward our new option.

Perhaps the decision will be unpopular or uncomfortable, but, deeper down, is there peace? Is your heart charged with God's energy? If so, then move forward with the decision, knowing that all has been done to discern God's desires.

Questions for Reflection

1. What are ways you pray outside of Mass?
2. Do you read the Bible? What are the advantages of praying with Scripture?
3. How do you breathe life into your prayer life?

Sources

Buckley, Michael. *The Catholic Prayer Book*. Cincinnati: Servant, 2013.

Hahn, Scott. "The Creed: Gateway to Grace," *Catholic Update*, September 2009.

Hays, Edward. "An Invitation to Prayer: A Guide for Deepening our Prayer Life," *Catholic Update*, February 1992.

Hutchinson, Gloria. "Our Father: The Prayer Jesus Taught Us," *Catholic Update*, December 1996.

_____. "The Rosary: A Prayer for All Seasons," *Catholic Update*, August 2003.

McCloskey, Pat, O.F.M. "How to Handle Anger With God," *Catholic Update*, July 1990.

Pope Benedict XVI. "Praying the Our Father with the Pope: From Jesus of Nazareth," *Catholic Update*, September 2007.

Pope John Paul II. "The Rosary of the Virgin Mary," *Catholic Update*, January 2003.

Richstatter, Thomas, O.F.M. "Why I Go to Mass," *Catholic Update*, August 2002.

Thibodeaux, Mark E., S.J. "Praydreaming: Key to Discernment," *Catholic Update*, February 2010.

Thompson, Thomas A., S.M., and Jack Wintz, O.F.M. "The Rosary: A Gospel Prayer," *Catholic Update*, May 1989.

Wilkes, Paul. "Seven Secrets of Successful Parishioners," *Catholic Update*, August 2004.

Wintz, Jack, O.F.M. "Pathways to Prayer," *Catholic Update*, March 1981.

_____. "The Luminous Mysteries: Exploring Five Major Events in Jesus' Public Ministry," *Catholic Update*, May 1989.

_____. "The Way of the Cross: A Lenten Devotion for Our Times," *Catholic Update*, February 1988.

Witherup, Ronald D., S.S. "Choosing and Using a Bible: What Catholics Should Know," *Catholic Update*, July 2004.

Zagano, Phyllis. "Examen of Consciousness: Finding God in All Things," *Catholic Update*, March 2003.

Contributors

Msgr. Michael Buckley has been parish priest in England and has worked full-time in the healing ministry. He is the compiling editor of *The Catholic Prayer Book*.

Dr. Scott Hahn, professor of theology and Scripture at Franciscan University in Steubenville, Ohio, since 1990, is a popular speaker, teacher, and author. He is the founder and director of the St. Paul Center for Biblical Theology and, in 2005, was appointed as the Pope Benedict XVI Chair of Biblical Theology and Liturgical Proclamation at St. Vincent Seminary in Latrobe, Pennsylvania.

Edward Hays is the author of more than thirty books on contemporary spirituality. He is the cofounder of Forest of Peace Publishing, served as director of Shantivanam, a Midwest center for contemplative prayer, and as a chaplain of the state penitentiary in Lansing, Kansas.

Gloria Hutchinson is a former teacher and catechist, an author and retreat director who writes extensively on the spiritual life. Her books include *Praying the Rosary; A Retreat With Teresa of Avila: Living by Holy Wit; Six Ways to Pray From Six Great Saints;* and *Praying the Way: Reflections on the Stations of the Cross.*

Pat McCloskey, O.F.M., is the Franciscan editor of *St. Anthony Messenger* magazine and author of *Day by Day with Followers of Francis and Clare* and the editor of revised editions of *Saint of the Day.*

Thomas Richstatter, O.F.M., a priest with a doctorate in liturgy and sacramental theology, is a popular writer and lecturer at St. Meinrad (Indiana) School of Theology.

Mark E. Thibodeaux, S.J., serves as novice director for Jesuits in formation and is an acknowledged expert on the topic of prayer and discernment. He is a well-known speaker and the author of *Armchair Mystic; God, I Have Issues: 50 Ways to Pray No Matter How You Feel;* and *God's Voice Within.*

Father Thomas Thompson, S.M., is director of the Marian Library at the University of Dayton and serves on the faculty of the International Research Institute and has served as secretary of the Mariological Society of America and editor of *Marian Studies* for more than twenty years.

Paul Wilkes is one of America's most respected writers and lecturers on religious belief and personal spirituality. The author of more than twenty books, and the host, writer, director, or producer of seven PBS documentaries, his book, *In Due Season: A Catholic Life*, was chosen by *Publishers Weekly* as one of 2009's one hundred outstanding books. His book *In Mysterious Ways: The Death and Life of a Parish Priest* was a Book-of-the-Month Club selection.

Jack Wintz, O.F.M., is the senior editor of *Catholic Update* and editor emeritus of *St. Anthony Messenger* magazine. The Franciscan friar is the author of Friar Jack's E-Spirations, *Will I See My Dog in Heaven?, St. Anthony of Padua: His Life, Legends, and Devotions,* and *Friar Jack's Favorite Prayers.*

Ronald D. Witherup, S.S., is provincial of the Sulpician Fathers, former Professor of Sacred Scripture at St. Patrick Seminary, Menlo Park, California, a prolific author, and a frequent contributor to American Catholic Radio. He is the author of *St. Paul, Called to Conversion: A Seven-Day Retreat.*

Phyllis Zagano is an author and frequent contributor to *National Catholic Reporter*. She has taught at Fordham, Boston, and Hofstra Universities. She has received awards for her books *Holy Saturday* and *Women & Catholicism.* In 2009, she was a Fulbright Fellow to the Republic of Ireland, and, in 2012, she received the Voice of the Faithful Saint Catherine of Siena Distinguished Layperson Award.